VIOLET

NEHA TIWARI

To my Coffee

Contents

Contents

Contents

1. A drop of blood

A drop of blood,
On my shirt,
My hands and legs,
Full of dirt,
Did nothing,
Just killed a jerked,

2. I miss those old days

I miss those old days,
When you used to care me,
Sleeping on your lap,
Taking a sweet nap,
Those days were mine,
I still have that,
Seeing you fading away,
But I still love you,
The way I used to be,
Its not easy to let you go,
I love you let me just show,
I miss those old days where I cannot go,

3. Knief in my hand

Knife in my hand,
Blood on the wall,
The hall was big,
The guy was tall,
I did something wrong,
He was in pain all along,
He died on the spot,
I regret it a lot,

4. Now and then

Now you are getting old,
My love for you,
Is still the same.
Can you love me?
The way you use to do,
Can you come back
Just for me?

5. All in my head

It was all in my head,
I was lying on my bed,
Neither I was alive,
Nor I was dead.
My heart was escaping my chest,
I was controlling,
I did my best!
Heart in pain,
Including the brain,
This thing cannot be explained.

6. She was good

I'm looking so nice today,
But my friend
Dares to say,
Her fair pointy chin,
I did it,
I grabbed my pin,
I threw my arm,
At her throat,
Covering her in,
Deep red blood.
Have told me at least
But now she is dead,
Rest in peace.

7. Cabin

Find the cabin,
Open the book
This is where she will look.
Trapped in daylight,
You see the pale light,
Burn your surroundings,
Bury then in blood,
Rain will pour down,
Thick like flood.

8. Grandma

Her old grey hair,
Playing with the air
Her old wrinkled face,
Full of grace
Her soft pink lips,
Chanting all god's clips.
She is unique,
She is mystique,
More than any antique.

9. Together

You play the drums,
I play the violin,
You play my heart
I play your soul
See, together we make
A whole.

10. So long

For a beautiful, blazing bold
And a warm spring day,
I feel so alone,
The fact that I waited so long.

11. Dead?

You are almost dead,
You don't have a pulse,
And your pillow
Is red,
Your family is gone,
Your friends let
You bleed,
Sleep with a knife dead,
That's all you need.

12. Sweetness

I thought you like me,
The sweetness you gave,
Like a heaven
It feels,
Your eyes make my heart fly,
Everything was good,
Until I cried

13. She saw her life

She saw her life,
She thought she,
She cannot survive.
The reason why she is alive,
Is leaving her side,
You think she is alight?
She is dying inside,
It's just she saw her life,
And thought she cannot survive.

14. All those friends

She killed them,
Without any regret,
She wasn't upset,
They all deserved it.
Shh!!
Don't make noise,
Someone will hear your voice.
Wrapped in the blanket,
They were crushed like toys.
She wasn't upset
As they all deserved it.

15. Scars

I hide my scars,
You touch them,
Telling me,
They feel like gem!

16. Cuts

My wrist, my blade
Blood across the floor,
A stroke of dripping down,
Thoughts of guilt
Now it's all over,
My canvas full of blood,
Naked body with all those cuts

17. I am!

I'm the king, I'm the queen,
"But you are just sixteen!"
"Dad took the lead,
He was just fifteen"
It's my turn to learn,
To be the king,
To be the queen
I'll use the sword,
I'll ride the horse,
I'll lead my force,
Coz,
I'll be the king,
I'll be the queen.

18. I met you as a dare

I met you as a dare,
But the soul that is you,
I couldn't share.
I was confused,
I keep walking away,
I still don't understand,
But I keep tracing back to you,
Obsession,
A sweet addiction,
There are things I needed,
To hear from you,
Like where I was fated,
Or the things you hated.
I put some shades on,
Strange is the fetish,
That turns me on
But now there's no confusion
No stepping back
I'll stick to you,
Coz,
Meeting you was a sweet dare.

19. She

She was having long pretty hair,
She cut is down,
And changed herself,
For the crown.

20. Fine

She is like a spring flower,
In the garden,
Trying to shine,
Pretending to be fine.

21. That day

That day,
The garden was filled
With lovely essence.
It was not because of the blossoms,
But because of your presence

22. Oh! my heart

Earth below,
Sky above,
I'll give you my heart,
Filled with love.

23. Trapped

I feel sad
I feel trapped,
But everything was
As usual as it was!
The same blue sky,
The same pain and cry,
The same people around,
The fear counts.
Something was gone,
Absolutely wrong.
Feeling sad,
Feeling trapped,
Everything was so crapped.

24. Soul and Body

Body without a soul,
OR
Soul without a body,
Both Searching for something.

25. Oh! my tear

Oh my tear!
Don't be my fear,
They way you roll down my cheek,
Sliding endlessly,
That's so unfair.

26. Lost

She is lost,
Lost on they she can never
Be found,
She is scared of
All those unknown
Sounds,
Following her all the way
Along.
She is strong,
Walking all alone.

27. Dear past

Oh! Dear past,
Don't be that harsh,
Already going through enough,
Things are tough.
Oh, dear past!

28. Everything in you

I really miss you,
You may not have a clue,
But I really do.
Your smile
Your Laugh,
Everything in you

29. Changed

She became quiet,
She stopped talking,
She started lying,
She was trying,
She was dying,
Sitting alone,
She was crying.
I miss her smile,
It was basically mine,
I know,
She wasn't fine,
She was trying,
She was dying
Sitting alone,
She was crying.
Red swollen eyes,
She was entering the dark side,
To come back to life,
She has to decide,
She was trying
She was dying
Sitting alone,

She was crying.
She hated humans,
She wasn't evil,
She was just struggling
At last,one
She is still trying
Still dying..........

30. All the happiness was gone

Everything I did,
Sems wrong,
All the happiness was gone,
Tried reading something,
Tried a song,
It wasn't enough,
As all the happiness was gone

31. Nightmare

When dreams fail,
To save you,
Nightmare grasp you,
You feel like drowning,
You feel like dying

32. You

You are the first thing I think of
Each morning,
When I rise,
You are the last thing I think of,
Each night,
Before I close my eyes,
You are every thought I have,
Every breath I take,
Every situation I face.

Chapter 33

I'd love it,
If you'd hold me tight,
I'd love it,
If you'd wish me
Good night,
I'd just love it
If you'd talk to me
The whole night,
I'd love it
If you'd just stay.

34. My world

My world,
Is for you,
Everything in you,
Belongs to you,
Do you have a clue?
How much I deserve you

35. The shines of life

The shines of life,
Never gonna be fine,
The faces shines,
But never gonna be fine,
Have to walk miles,
Coz shines of life,
Never gonna be fine,

36. Heart and brain

Heart and brain,
Tolerating the pain,
Crying in the corner,
Crying in the Rain,
Hide my scars,
They aren't stars.

37. Blue eyes

She was afraid
Of the ocean,
It was dark,
Deep,
Endless motion,
But when she saw,
Those blue eyes,
She knew
She will not die.

38. Before I die

Oh! My,
Before I die,
The thought of death,
Makes me cry,
Oh! My,
But why not,
I should try,
To do something
Amazing,
Before I die,
Oh! Dear
So many things,
So little time,
What should I do,
Before I die,
So many things to think
Of,
Too many things
To do,
Oh! My
Before I die.

39. Her

Her love was an angel
Everyday was a new hell,
Her pillows were,
Covered in tears,
She lived in fear,
It wasn't worth
The pain,
It caused her,
To be insane.

40. Surviving

The reason for being
Alive,
She is trying to survive,
She wants that back,
The one,
She is losing track.

41. I'm Toxic

We all crash and burn,
I'm toxic,
You have to learn,
This is all I can say,
You have to be away.

42. Don't leave

I cut deeper every day,
But the scars never,
Stay,
On my wrist,
Are your lies,
To show my,
Cries,
I can't handle,
If you leave,
All I feel is grief.

43. Pills

I failed,
What a shame,
Those pills
Couldn't erase,
My name,
Two weeks in a room,
I'm crazy,
That's what they assume,
That one pill,
Wasn't enough,
Life was just so tough.

44. Venus

And to think,
I couldn't stay away,
From you for more than a day,
I don't deserve you,
Or The happiness,
But little did I know,
You are my Venus

45. Hear my voice

Hear my voice,
Dead red,
Full of blood,
O dear,
Its not my choice,
Here my voice here my voice,

46. Red and Blue

Roses are red,

Violets are blue,

This is few,

All for you

You might not

Have a clue

But it's true,

I know, it's

doesn't matter for you,

47. Just her

Her mind is worse,
Her life is a curse,
Her heart is lie,
She better say goodbye

48. It won't get better

It won't get better,
It won't be okay,
It will still stay the same,
Day by day,
My mind's a gameplay
Cutting me deeper and deeper,
Everyday,
Just be away,
That's what i pray

49. Sins

I cascade into darkness
I rip into skin,
I fight for my life,
I cry beneath my sins,
My mind is never going to win

50. A thousand Times

It creeps alone,
Swallows inside,
It screams at you,
A thousand times

51. Thoughts

She taste the pills
Sliding down her throat,
She feel the cuts,
Slicing through,
Her skin,
She hear the thoughts,
screaming in her head,
She catch the wave,
Slowing sinking her.

52. Burning heart

My burning heart,
My sorrowful sin,
My lifeless body,
In the bin.
My red stained skin,
And my wet,
Fresh blood,
The blood in which,
Starts the flood,
My tears that,
Stream down my face,
My tears that,
Stream down my face,
My depression greater,
I have no place,
I need a new
Host,
For now,
I'm nothing
But a lonely ghost.

53. She was a star

She was a star
Twinkling up
so far,
Hiding all
her scars

54. Mark

Red
Blood
And Dead
This is what,
She said,
No clue left,
Just a mark
On the chest